Subparts of a Life

Subparts of a Life

40 STORIES ON
BEING HUMAN

Chris Ehrlich

1 Minute Stories

Also By Chris Ehrlich

Parts of a Life: 40 Stories on
Youth to Adulthood

CONTENTS

For Fiona, Scott, and James

Identity

He walks out of the locker room.
Football practice is over.

He's holding a black instrument case.
Holding his football gear.

He sees a man walking his direction.
Walking on the same path through campus.

He knows the man.
Talked with him before.

The man's retired.
Lives in a nearby neighborhood.

The man wears a baseball hat.
Eyeglasses.

The man holds a tennis ball.
Bounces it.

The man takes walks during football practices.
Watches a little.

The man sometimes makes remarks to him.
Passing along the field's edge.

Stay out of the mud, the man says.
That option play is clicking, the man says.

He responds.
That's how he knows.

That the man retired recently.
The doctor says he needs daily exercise.

That the days are long.
Walks are a good routine.

That the man carries a tennis ball.
For something to do on a long walk.

The man only talks to him.
No other players.

He's walking out of the practice grounds.
The man's walking in.

The two approach each other.
Slow for a greeting.

The man notices the black case.
Hanging at his side.

You play an instrument Mr. Quarterback, the man
says.
What do you play.

Violin, he says.
I'm not the best.

Violin, the man says.
I didn't know you're a Renaissance man.

There aren't too many of you anymore.

Passion

A group of students wait on benches.
Idle in a main hallway after school.

They're quiet.
Unbothered.

He's dirty from practice.
His hair is a mess.

Have you ever had one of these muffins.
He asks everyone.

Some kids look at him.
Showing slight interest.

Where'd you get it from.
A kid asks.

I get them from that one frozen yogurt store.
Whenever I can.

They only have a handful every day.
Sometimes I go, and they're out.

I even call them sometimes.
To see if they have any.

I really shouldn't be telling you about them.
They sell out all the time.

What flavors do they have.
A kid asks.

You have to get whatever flavor they have.
You can't expect any flavor being there.

They sell three flavors.
Blueberry, chocolate, and cinnamon.

They're kind of expensive.
But it's fair.

They're huge.
It's a lot of food.

It's a lot of calories too.
Probably not that great for you.

But it can't be that bad for you.
It's kind of a healthy place.

Oh my gosh, why do you like them so much.
A kid asks.

You're thinking they can't be that good.
I'm telling you they are.

They're not a regular baked good.
You can't find them anywhere else.

They're clearly made differently.
They're high-end.

The top is moist.
The bottom is cake-like but still moist.

None of it is dry.
That's a big reason.

Whatever flavor you do get.
They're serious about it.

Blueberry.
It's all these different shapes.

Chocolate.
It's chocolate everywhere.

Cinnamon.
It's the perfect amount.

And when you're done with the top.
The flavor's not all gone.

They put chunks of flavor in the bottom.
So there's a reason to the bottom.

That's not normal.
Usually, the flavor's gone after the top.

The bottom is just there.
Not even worth having.

Then you have the wrapper.
That's a big part of the experience.

It's this plastic wrap.
That goes all around it.

If you want to save some of it.
Or you have to go.

You can re-seal it.
And take it with you.

There's no mess.
Ever.

The crumbs help you out too.
They're somehow big.

You just grab them from the wrapper.
Before they fall anywhere.

Do you ever just get their frozen yogurt.
A kid asks.

I never get anything else.
It's why I go there.

I always get their gourmet muffin.

A girl asks about him the next day.
A schoolmate tells him what she said.

She asked who's that boy.
The boy who was talking after practice.

Okay, he says.
Why.

She wants me to give you her number.
She said she's never heard anyone talk that way
about a muffin.

She's never heard anyone talk that way about
anything.

3

Discipline

He stays after football practice to practice.
To throw the football.

He recruits a wide receiver to stay.
One who wants to get better.

The practice field is empty.
The team is in the locker room.

He asks them to line up.
Says which route to run.

Ready, set, go.
He drops back.

They run the route.
Swiftly.

He throws the ball at them.
They catch it.

They jog toward him.
Toss the ball back.

Nice route.
Good catch.

He stays back from the line.
For them to recover.

Let's run it again.
A few more times.

Turn your head early.
As you break.

They line up.
Looking over.

Ready, set, go.
He drops back.

They run the route.
Swiftly.

He throws the ball at them.
They catch it.

They jog toward him.
Toss the ball back.

Nice.
That's the right timing.

He stays back from the line.
For them to recover.

This one will be a second later.
Keep moving forward to the ball.

They line up.
Looking over.

Ready, set, go.
He drops back.

They run the route.
Swiftly.

He throws the ball at them.
They catch it.

They jog toward him.
Toss the ball back.

Nice.
That's key if the ball isn't there yet.

He calls more routes.
They run more routes.

It's a performance.
The playbook's passing plays.

He practices until he feels done.
Until it gets darker.

He wonders if he stops.
Will it matter.

He trusts it will matter.
Someday.

The repetition.
Repeated.

In the summer.
After practices.

When he doesn't have to.
There's no rule.

When nothing changes.
There's no payoff.

When he's not sure why.
There's no reason.

He expects it.
A duty to himself.

Unglorified.
No promises.

He does the drill.
Again.

He does the unseen.

4

Opportunity

His dad is talking on the phone.
In the kitchen.

He hears his dad call out.
Your brother wants to talk with you.

His dad waits.
He takes the phone.

He's at home on a break from college.
A senior at a school near Columbus, Ohio.

His older brother's been away for a couple years.
Living in San Francisco, California.

What are you doing after graduation, his brother
says.
Do you know.

Yeah, sort of, he says.
I'll go wherever I get a good job.

Or I'll go to Columbus.
It's a great city. I like it.

Another idea is Charleston.
South Carolina.

I'd go there to write.
To move south.

Okay, I get those, his brother says.
Those sound pretty good.

You should think about coming to San Francisco.
And living with me.

I have a room.
I could keep it for you.

San Francisco is a real city.
You'll love it.

It's so different.
You almost need to live here for a while.

His brother continues.
Enthused.

Okay, I'll definitely think about it, he says.
I'll let you know what I'm doing.

They hang up.
He sits at the kitchen table.

Recalls what he said.
What his brother said.

Knowing soon.
He does graduate.

He's never thought about San Francisco.
It's not his idea.

It's his brother's city.
Not his.

Charleston is tempting.
Not now.

Columbus is more the idea.
He can't.

He's certain he'd meet someone.
Certain he'd stay there.

It isn't time.
To know what happens.

Unmoved.
He corrects himself.

He's being absent.
Discourteous.

To say no to San Francisco.
Would be saying no to life.

He'd like to know life.
See what it wants to show him.

Though sudden.
Though bold.

He's holding life's invitation.

5

Independence

He leaves his apartment building.
Walks on the sidewalk.

The sidewalk can take him anywhere.
He's in San Francisco, California.

He graduated college two months ago.
Half a country away.

He's walking to work.
He could take the bus.

It's a fine day.
He has time.

He wants to see his new city.
The people of his city.

He walks by other apartment buildings.
Their understated entrances a touch ornate.

Few people are walking.
Luxury cars hum on the street.

He knows it isn't home.
It's temporary.

He turns.
Walks downhill toward downtown.

He passes a bagel shop.
His favorite spot.

Working people in between work.
Older people stepping out.

He walks up a hill.
Climbs for blocks.

He passes townhomes by a park.
A flowing fountain in the center.

People wearing designer jackets.
Leather gloves.

He reaches level ground.
A grand hotel with stone columns.

Travelers emerge.
Talk in foreign languages.

He turns downhill past an art college.
Students line the street.

Smoking.
Gesturing.

Speaking about art.
Looking at him.

He passes a block of hotels.
Along a fashion square.

Doormen in formal hats stand in front.
Direct drivers.

They carry bags.
Show the city works.

The smallest pizza shop takes orders.
People wait in line on the sidewalk.

He smells fresh pizza slices.
Why doesn't he eat there more.

A seven-story department store draws shoppers.
Tourists plan what's next by subway stairs.

He walks through the crowd.
A reminder he lives in a city people visit.

He passes a bakery with patio seating.
Where he lunches sometimes.

Women around his age eat there.
He may talk with one.

He approaches the building where he works.
Art is chiseled into the walls.

A tower rises from its corner.
A clock turns at the top.

A flag pole rises from the tower.
An American flag flies above.

Will he ever be as great as the building he enters.
The city around it.

Before he can be someone.
He can be anyone.

He can walk alone.

6

Curiosity

She's standing in an apartment.
Next to a man in the living room.

She doesn't know him.
He's a friend of a friend.

The hosts are offering drinks.
Appetizers.

The sun is setting.
They'll all stay a while.

Most everyone is talking.
Seats are taken.

She's not interested in him.
He's not interested in her.

"What part of the city do you live in?" she says.

He says a neighborhood.
She comments on his neighborhood.

She waits.
He's silent.

"Where are you from?" she says.

He says a hometown.
She comments on his hometown.

She waits.
He's silent.

"Why did you move to the city?" she says.

He says a few reasons.
She comments on the reasons.

She waits.
He's silent.

She sees a chance to spur him.
An interest of his.

He's wearing loud sneakers.
They don't match his outfit.

The sneakers are a statement.
His fashion.

"What kind of sneakers are those?" she says.
"Where did you get them?"

He's activated.
Talks in sneaker terms.

He continues.
Unasked.

Talks about his types of sneakers.
Why he needs a variety.

"How do you decide which pair to wear?" she says.
"With each outfit?"

He lists different occasions.
The right sneakers.

He talks about his current outfit.
Why he picked the pair he's wearing.

She asks more.
A study of male fashion.

He explains further.
She comments on the sneaker lesson.

People are shifting in the room.
Spots are opening.

She decides to end the uneven exchange.
To ask him nothing else.

"Well, you have a good night," she says.
"I'll look for your sneakers next time."

He says something similar.
Oblivious to himself.

He doesn't ask anyone a question all night.

7

Wonder

He walks on a sidewalk.
In San Francisco, California.

His old school friend is with him.
Visiting the city from far away.

They could go anywhere to eat.
Fine restaurants are everywhere.

His friend loves fine restaurants.
Trying different foods.

Their walk is for another delicacy.
Less regarded.

They're walking to a bagel shop.
The one he frequents.

He has to take his friend there.
To get the shop's apple fritter.

To taste the real city.
He wouldn't bring everyone there.

Not everyone can see it.
It's personal.

His friend can.
Can see what he sees.

The shop isn't noticed.
Despite regular signs.

There are high chairs.
Around high tables.

Along a set of windows.
Where two streets meet.

They get the same orders.
He insists.

A toasted everything bagel.
With cream cheese.

An apple fritter.
A premium menu item.

A fountain soda pop.
Large.

They sit down.
By the window.

People are out.
On the sidewalks.

Walking to shop.
To eat.

Leaving home.
Coming home.

This place is perfect, his friend says.
I'd go here too.

They talk as they eat.
About family.

Cities.
Culture.

Who they are.
Who they aren't.

They joke.
About the fritter.

They laugh.
About a dog on the street.

Barking at them.
Their food.

About the dog entering the shop.
Sitting beside them.

It's how they were years ago.
They laughed at everything.

They had to.
Everything was amazing.

Shop names.
Menus.

Each other.
Anyone around them.

Their schoolmates.
Teammates.

They clean the table.
Throw out the trash.

Say thanks to the worker.
Wave as they leave.

You're right, his friend says.
That has to be the best apple fritter ever.

They step on to the street.
To explore more of San Francisco.

Looking together.
For hours.

What else is incredible in the city.

8

Presence

She walks into a friend's house.
Greets everyone inside.

The friend and her husband are hosting dinner.
For two other couples.

It's her first time meeting one of the husbands.
Her husband's met him before.

They all sit on the deck.
Under a warm summer sky.

Some are wearing sandals.
It's a casual affair.

They share cheese.
Crackers.

They sip their drinks.
Different kinds.

They hear dinner is prepared.
Walk into the kitchen.

The husband she doesn't know is ahead of her.
He hands her a plate.

They all return to the deck.
Plates in their laps.

They talk about the meal.
He's silent.

He smiles some.
Laughs some.

They talk about kids.
He's silent.

Someone asks for an extra napkin.
He offers his.

They talk about marriage.
He's silent.

He gets up.
Asks if anyone needs anything from inside.

They talk about exercise.
He's silent.

He nods his head.
In agreement.

They talk about leisure.
He's silent.

He takes his empty plate to the kitchen.
Gathers a couple empty plates on the way.

The sky is dark.
It's cool.

The host couple says it's time for bed.
They all say their goodbyes.

Her husband opens the car door for her.
They drive back home.

He asks about him.
The one she hadn't met.

What do you think of him, he says.
I like his energy.

I don't know, she says.
He certainly seems nice.

Do you not like him, he says.
What did he do.

No, she says.
He didn't do anything.

I just don't think he said a word.

9

Respect

He hears his father-in-law.
Calling his name.

Asking for help with a chore.
Putting a car cover on a car.

The car's in the driveway.
Among a forest.

He's visiting his in-laws.
With his wife and kids.

He knows what's been asked.
Who asked it.

He rises.
Walks to the driveway.

A recruit.
At attention.

His father-in-law knows the cover.
Used it many times before.

His father-in-law knows what works.
What doesn't.

He's helped with the cover before.
Forgettable showings.

His father-in-law handles the cover.
Heaves it across the car.

His father-in-law instructs.
He listens.

He grabs his half.
Pulls it toward him.

His father-in-law stretches.
Secures his half.

He stretches.
Strains to secure his half.

His father-in-law walks along one side.
Tucks along the lines.

He walks along the other side.
Looks for lines to tuck.

His father-in-law checks the cover.
Fixes two subpar spots.

Thank you, his father-in-law says.
Of course, he says.

The car is well covered.
He walks back inside.

Humbled by the chore.
By re-encountering his wife's father.

A man who deserves.
At the least.

His most fumbling salute.

10

Gregarious

His house is full of guests.
He's not friends with any of them.

He's hosting a holiday party with his wife.
Their kids.

Their guests are neighbors.
Neighborhood kids.

Parents of schoolmates.
Schoolmates.

It's an exclusive affair.
Every invitation was discussed.

The adults don't know each other.
Talk about themselves to each other.

They eat the food he just bought.
Drink the drinks he just bought.

They stand together in rooms.
Sit together on couches.

They find an unexpected spot.
By a tree in the back yard.

He talks with all of them.
Personalizes each approach.

He talks more with some.
Those who speak.

He appreciates one guy.
The one with no ego.

He learns about the unknown adults.
If they have good energy.

He checks the food.
The drinks.

The kids know each other.
Say whatever they want to each other.

They hop through the house.
Not yet inhibited.

They make art with fresh art supplies.
Play with forgotten toys.

They play with a ball outside.
Change the rules.

He directs kids looking for kids.
Kids looking for another option.

Their kids re-discover their home.
Friends.

He learns about the unknown kids.
Where they fit in the group.

He sees his wife smiling.
Guests asking about her.

He gets closer to hear.
What will she say.

She talks about the past.
Her younger self.

A family leaves early.
Others stay longer.

Some guests visit him.
Say thank you.

He starts cleaning.
His wife starts cleaning.

Their kids keep playing.
Neighborhood kids stay around.

She stops to enjoy a bite of food.
Consider the empty house.

He stops beside her.
She waits.

He asks why they don't host more parties.

11

Selflessness

He removes clothes from their bedroom closet.
Clothes he doesn't wear.

His wife removes clothes from their bedroom
closet.
Clothes from different cities.

They remove their shoes from the closet.
Shoes that were their fashion.

They remove their clothes from the dressers.
Clothes from other times.

They remove their lamps.
Lamps they picked as newlyweds.

They remove their books.
Books they like near them.

They remove their picture frames.
Pictures of them together.

They speak only about the room.
What they're doing.

They sweep the hardwood floor.
Taking turns.

They get on their knees.
Scrub several spots.

They clean the walls.
The windows.

They look around the room.
They're done.

He stands at each window.
Shows his wife the views.

Look at the tree branches.
The sidewalks below.

Look at the rooftops.
The clouds past them.

They walk downstairs to their younger son.
He's playing in the family room.

They want to show him something.
They walk him upstairs to their bedroom.

This is your new room, his wife says.
Like we talked about.

You and your brother have your own rooms now.

12

Responsibility

He walks upstairs.
Becomes a dad.

He can't show them anything.
Where his mind goes.

Not his strain.
Frustration.

His present.
Near future.

His uncertainty.
Determination.

It's not their concern.
Not their game.

He shields them.
They don't know.

Do this well.
Give.

He enters the rooms of his three kids.
It's bedtime.

He asks each one about their day.
Stays with them.

He stands.
Sits in a chair.

He talks with them.
Offers counsel.

He says the bobcat doesn't want to be alone.
They welcome its new spot.

Here's this fun book for later.
They tilt the cover to judge it.

What can you learn from this trading card.
They examine one side.

He hugs them.
Says goodnight.

He walks to the doorway.
Looks at them.

He proclaims their name.
Praises them for something.

He closes the door.
Walks downstairs.

His reality is waiting.
Shadows find him.

He sits on a couch.
Copes with the night.

A boy once.
A young man for a time.

He must keep trying.
Find his way.

His kids are just starting to dream.

13

Fun

He makes a decision.
He's been thinking about it.

He walks out of his house.
Drives across town.

He parks in a shopping center.
Enters a sporting goods store.

He passes nice clothes.
Sneakers.

Nice sports gear.
Accessories.

He turns to his section.
The tennis rackets.

He notices one he likes.
Not the latest model.

Yellow.
Black.

Once used by a top player.
Known for their fight.

He holds it.
Swings it.

His strokes aren't tour level.
He needs to practice.

The cashier says it's a great racket.
Hands him the overdue possession.

He places it beside him in the car.
Where he can admire it.

He turns up the music.
Drives home.

Is it true.
He's going to start playing again.

He played some as a boy.
Group lessons in the summer.

He loved it.
Sometimes he sees himself then.

Running around.
Hitting tennis balls.

Where did he go.
He doesn't know.

He's been looking for him.
Without a clue for years.

His new racket is a trace of what was.
Telling him he's closer to that boy.

The boy who was always smiling.

14

Kindness

His son's friend climbs into the back seat.
His son follows him.

They're in baseball uniforms.
He's driving them to a game.

He says hi to the friend.
It's good to see you.

He plays pop music on the radio.
A soundtrack for the boys.

He listens to the boys talk.
Listens for a break.

He asks the friend which classes he likes.
What are you doing for fun.

He asks what his siblings are doing.
How is your mom doing.

He watches their baseball game.
Cheers for them.

He hands them cash after.
The snack shack is still open.

They share candy in the car.
Defend their drink choices.

He tells his son beautiful hit.
Tells the friend amazing catch.

He plays pop music on the radio.
The boys sing to a song.

He asks if they want some food.
They say they want to get home.

They play in his son's room.
Outside for a while.

They keep playing.
He lets them play late.

He calls them in for a popsicle.
Says they can take the friend home.

He sits down with them.
Eats a popsicle.

He asks his son what they played.
Asks the friend what else they played.

He turns into the friend's driveway.
Turns to the back seat.

He says it was so great seeing you.
You can come over anytime.

His son says goodbye.
Smiles at the friend's exit.

They watch the friend find his house key.
Wave in his baseball uniform.

He says he likes helping the friend.
Likes helping the friend's mom.

She's always so good to you.
She's always treating you.

Isn't she.

15

Commitment

He disagrees with his wife.
She disagrees with him.

They disagree more.
Until it's clear they disagree.

They're not pleased with each other.
Quiet in different rooms.

He continues with his evening.
Going to the supermarket.

He asks if she wants anything.
An initial truce.

She tells him some items.
He writes them down.

She settles into a couch.
He leaves to the store.

He walks the aisles.
Finds her items.

He grabs them off shelves.
Puts them in the shopping cart.

He knows one of them isn't there.
It's at a store nearby.

He goes to the next store.
Finds her other item.

He waits to pay.
Sees a display of candy bars.

He focuses on one.
His wife's favorite.

When did he last buy her one.
When did she last have one.

He's not sure.
Is this the day to get her one.

He gets her favorite candy bar.
Returns home.

He enters.
Calls to her.

I got everything you wanted, he says.
Thank you, she says.

He unpacks the grocery items.
Puts them away in the kitchen.

She's on the couch.
He walks over to her.

Here.
I got you this too.

Oh. That's nice.
I don't need it but thank you.

I know you don't.
You're welcome.

It's not for her.
The chocolate offering.

It's for their marriage.

16

Intensity

He walks on a tennis court.
Alone.

It's sunny.
93 degrees.

He's practicing his strokes.
All of them.

Doing exercise.
A mental game.

He stands up a metal basket.
Full of tennis balls.

He looks at his clock.
He'll be there a while.

He takes 1 ball.
Puts 2 others in his pocket.

He bounces the ball.
Hits a forehand.

He hits more forehands.
Makes adjustments.

To his arms.
His racket.

His legs.
His feet.

8 minutes later.
He hits the basket's last ball.

His meditation.
Underway.

He walks to the other side.
Balls cover the court.

He picks up the balls.
Re-fills the basket.

He hits baskets of forehands.
Baskets of forehand slices.

He begins to drip sweat.
Move slower.

He hits baskets of backhands.
Baskets of backhand slices.

Sunrays are defeating him.
A hat is his defense.

He pictures a cold drink after.
Food.

He hits baskets of serves.
Baskets of different serves.

His body's breaking down.
As desired.

He looks at his clock.
Could've stopped long ago.

He's close.
Almost extreme.

At 3 hours.
He stops.

He bags his racket.
Releases his fixation.

He picks up the balls.
Hobbles off the tennis court.

He's weak.
Broken.

More alive.

17

Generosity

He looks up at a bakery's menu.
His dad looks up at the menu.

He's a middle-aged man.
With kids.

His dad is an older man.
With grandkids.

His dad likes the bakery.
It's one of his favorite places.

He's in town.
Out with his dad.

His dad orders.
Say thanks to the worker.

Do you know what you want, his dad says.
Get something good.

Okay, he says.
Thanks Dad.

He orders.
Says thanks to the worker.

He finds a good table.
His dad joins him.

His dad re-endorses the bakery.
He agrees.

He rises to pick up their orders.
Returns with a tray.

He has a bagel.
Tea.

His dad has a sandwich.
Soup.

He takes a sip of tea.
His dad asks about him.

He talks.
His dad supports him.

He asks about his dad.
Bites into the bagel.

His dad's response is direct.
Honest.

He asks his dad anything.
His dad shares experiences.

His dad asks him anything.
He tells his dad.

He takes more sips.
His dad takes more bites.

Their plates become empty.
He clears the table.

His dad heads toward the exit.
He follows.

Thank you Dad, he says.
For the bagel and the tea.

You're welcome son, his dad says.
It's nothing.

He strides through the air outside.
His sneakers gripping the parking lot.

A fit man.
An aging athlete.

Capable as he is.
He knows.

He'll always be thanking his dad.

18

Objectivity

He walks in a park.
On a paved trail.

His two teenage sons walk with him.
His wife.

They have their greyhound.
A bag of balls.

The boys are playing catch.
Throwing a toy football.

They walk winding paths.
Reach a straightaway.

When did he last race the boys.
It was on a beach.

They were different ages.
He beat both of them.

The boys are sporting.
He says let's race.

Let's see if you can beat me.
It should be close.

He gets a stick.
Marks the starting line.

His wife stands at the finish line.
50 yards away.

She'll signal the start.
Judge the winner.

They line up.
One of the boys false starts.

They line up again.
Everyone behind the line.

His wife raises her arm to drop it.
She yells on your mark, get set, go.

They're hauling.
No one wants to be last.

They hit full stride.
One passes another.

His older son finishes first.
His younger son finishes second.

He finishes third.
Last.

His wife says it wasn't a photo finish.
Announces the placers.

It's his first loss to the boys.
Ever.

He's stunned by his bronze.
Deflated.

He says he's not in form.
He'd like a re-match one day.

They dismiss him.
The last-place sprinter.

It's their time to be fast.

19

Introspection

I drive to the supermarket.
My family needs me to go.

I follow the route.
See if I like my city.

I hear a song on the radio.
Remember when I had expectations.

I park.
Walk toward the store.

The weather tries to persuade me.
I ask the sky for more.

I'm under-dressed for the supermarket.
For anywhere.

My outfit is out of fashion.
Every piece.

I could look better.
Why aren't I interested in clothes.

My hair is brushed.
I don't mistreat hair.

My face is shaved.
I don't look good unshaved.

I move at will.
I could run at any moment.

I see holiday items on display.
Let's celebrate more this year.

A mom is stalled in an aisle.
She's raising two little kids.

I smile at her.
I was her years ago.

A focused man aims for one section.
He's on a mission.

I smile at him.
I've been him.

Two teenagers are being loud.
They have nowhere to be.

I smile at them.
I used to be them.

I walk from aisle to aisle.
How am I.

I should be fine.
I like this place.

I'm fine.
Nothing followed me in.

Am I strolling.
Go slower.

I pick our last item from a shelf.
Is it healthy.

I pay for my family's haul.
Bags of good fortune.

I push my cart around moving cars.
Start to smile outside.

I haven't changed.

20

Support

He finds a row in a theater.
A play's about to begin.

He sits on the left side.
Near the front.

He'd like a fresh perspective.
He's seen the play twice.

On opening night.
He sat in the center.

The night before.
He sat on the right side.

The stage curtains open.
Act one starts.

He knows the story.
The plot.

He knows the cast.
What they say.

He knows the surprises.
The ending.

What did he miss before.
He'll look for it tonight.

He's there to watch one actor.
He knows her.

There she is.
Entering the stage.

The lights are on her.
She acts.

She's practiced.
A thespian.

She's interesting.
A character.

She's different.
The audience follows her.

He watches the audience.
Watching her.

She makes them laugh.
Laugh more.

She leaves the stage.
He waits for her return.

He admires the sets.
The costumes.

He considers the actors.
Their portrayals.

There she is.
The script calls for her.

As a traveler.
A realist.

A force.
A storyteller.

She exits the stage.
The script calls for her no more.

The stage curtains close.
The show's over.

The actors emerge.
Take turns bowing.

He claps loudest for her.
Cheers loudest for her.

He walks to a hallway.
Actors are meeting fans.

She's in full costume.
Full stage makeup.

She's hugging people.
Complimented.

He stays back.
Waits nearby.

She sees him.
In her school's theater.

Dad, she says.
You didn't have to come tonight.

You're in the play, he says.
It's show week.

Nothing else matters.

21

Love

She talks with their dog.
Who's the best girl, she says.

Their greyhound is standing next to her.
Nestling their head on her leg.

She bends down.
Holds their head with both hands.

She looks into their eyes.
Who's the luckiest girl.

She walks to the closet.
Puts on her jacket.

They race over.
Ready for anything.

She grabs the leash.
Holds on to it.

They look up at her.
Do you know something girl.

She grabs the car keys.
Rattles them.

Do you want to go somewhere with me.
You better come on then.

She runs to the back door.
They dart behind her.

She leashes them.
They high step out the back door.

Her husband follows the pair outside.
To send-off his wife and greyhound.

She opens the car's back door.
Helps her best friend climb in.

She glides around to the driver's door.
Carefree.

He waves to each of them.
Blows a kiss.

They drive away.
Heading somewhere.

He stands beside the driveway.
A witness.

It becomes clear to him.
He understands.

Who his wife is.
What his wish is for her.

To only ever be this happy.

22

Risk

He and his wife round up the kids.
They have exciting news.

The kids arrive in the living room.
Sit on the couches.

He and his wife talked earlier.
Agree on what to say.

He remains standing.
Begins.

We know this is a great town.
We've always told you it is.

But we think you've grown.
Done all you can here.

We think you can grow more.
In a different type of town.

We're moving.
By the start of next school year.

The kids look around.
One declares they knew it.

We know it's horrible now.
Horrible for each of you.

But we know you'll become better people.
Being there.

Not soon.
In a few years.

You're going to be more balanced.
Have more perspective on yourself.

To make choices later.
To know life.

He talks about other reasons.
Issues they've heard before.

His wife begins.
Talks to the kids.

He looks to a screen nearby.
Ready with dozens of prepared images.

It's unusual.
Visual.

He says this is where we're moving.
Here's the state.

The city.
The area.

The school.
The sports.

The parks.
The arts.

He talks about each image.
His wife does the same.

The kids ask questions.
Some of the images stir them.

He says the move will make us better.
All of us.

Not now.
When you're older.

Have fun with everyone here now.
You're going to visit.

The kids respond.
Injured.

The gathering breaks.
The move is spoken.

He returns to the plan.
Complete destruction.

Destroying his family's present.
From within.

To create their future.

23

Wanting

She talks with her husband.
Shares her dreams.

She wants to make room for her art.
Make an art studio at home.

She wants to find a spot in the city.
Ask to paint a mural there.

She wants to exhibit her art.
Sell her art.

She talks with her friend.
Shares her ideas.

She wants to try that new restaurant.
The one by the water.

She wants to hike a state park.
Picnic along the way.

She wants to go downtown.
See the symphony.

She talks with her mom.
Shares her hopes.

She wants to teach art.
Technique.

She wants to find an arts center.
Become an instructor.

She wants to be around new artists.
Be around their energy.

He talks with his wife.
Shares his dreams.

He wants to write a book.
Write what he thinks.

He wants to publish the book.
Make it small.

He wants to get the book in libraries.
Where he lived.

His wife says okay.
Why.

He says he keeps thinking about an old friend.
A girl he knew in school.

She was his age.
She had a husband.

There must be so much she wanted to do.
So much she didn't do.

He thinks how she's not here anymore.
How he's still here.

How he needs to write his book this year.

24

Teaching

He's the pitcher.
His daughter is at bat.

She's 7.
Wearing her favorite hat.

Her younger brothers are outfielders.
Ready to field.

They're playing on a street.
A cul-de-sac with no traffic.

He pitches a plastic baseball.
She swings a plastic baseball bat.

She hits the ball.
All right, he says.

He has a bag of plastic baseballs.
Re-loads.

He pitches.
She hits the ball.

He pitches.
She hits the ball.

Wow, he says.
Keep hitting.

The boys run around the cul-de-sac.
Find the balls.

He pitches more to her.
She hits each ball.

Her power grows.
Balls are airborne.

Her hits fly into other yards.
Roll down distant driveways.

One brother yells.
You're going to lose all of our balls.

She can't miss.
You're a great hitter, he says.

Her batting technique is untraditional.
Her own.

He shows her a traditional swing.
She rejects it.

He raises the game.
Becomes a real pitcher.

Throws faster.
Throws junk balls.

She's unintimidated.
Unaffected.

She hits each ball.
Re-sets.

She doesn't smile.
Knows she's being challenged.

He admires each hit.
Where each ball ends up.

She's a natural.
He never tries to change her swing.

There are other days.
Days she exhibits her batting ability.

She gets older.
He keeps telling her.

You're a pure batter.
One of the best I've ever seen.

She doesn't play softball.
Baseball.

They aren't the plan.
Her plan.

Her batting days are in her.
Her strength.

She owns a metal baseball bat.
Hits better than ballplayers in gym class.

A woman.
She marches into a major city alone.

She visits him at home.
They talk about anything.

She mentions she's a great hitter.

25

Mission

His parents keep nice children's books at home.
Hardcovers.

Elementary school teachers hand him illustrated
books.
Books on how to imagine.

Middle school teachers assign him award-winning
books.
Books with medals on the covers.

High school teachers assign him contemporary
books.
Books studied by a nation.

College professors assign him classic books.
Books studied by the world.

He explores books at every bookstore.
Reads the back covers.

He's interested in the authors.
Who are they.

Are they mostly telling a story.
Perhaps they have something to say.

What's their premise.
Perhaps it isn't cliché.

Who's it for.
Perhaps it's for the genre.

Without the book.
There are no questions.

The book is real.
Not an idea.

However popular.
However unread.

The book is part of culture.
Part of history.

He respects the author's audacity.
Their commitment.

Their pages travel.
Their voice speaks.

Why not him, he thinks.
He can write.

He wants to say something.
His present is now.

He wants his words to live.
To outlast him.

He was here.
Here's what he thought.

What will he say.
What won't he say.

He mines his mind.
Discovers his stories.

He welcomes the hours.
Writes.

188 pages later.
He's done.

One book is enough, he thinks.
He'll be satisfied.

He's surprised.
By writing.

By how alive he is.
The unknown.

About missing it.
The play.

He learns he's not done.
He starts writing his next book.

He has more to say.

26

Resilience

He wakes up before sunrise.
He has to be somewhere.

He shaves his face.
Why.

There's flossing.
Brushing his teeth.

He selects an outfit.
Why.

There's showering.
Drying off.

He brushes his hair.
Why.

He heats a kettle.
Water for his travel tea mug.

A lingering gift.
He doesn't let go.

He eats his breakfast.
Prepared the night before.

The morning's hope.
Gone.

He puts personal items in a bag.
Something to do later.

He takes his lunch bag.
Prepared the night before.

The day's hope.
Something to look toward.

He walks out the door.
The street's asleep.

The highway's deserted.
He drives to another city.

He parks at a building.
Brings his bags.

He put himself there.
Destiny meeting him.

A few different decisions.
He's somewhere else.

He enters the building.
Passes security.

He must.
His options the same as yesterday.

He sees others.
There for different reasons.

It's time to do what he never imagined.
Never expected.

What he never trained for.
Never wanted.

It's his job.

27

Dream

He's in a bookstore.
Sitting at a table.

Among copies of his book.
Acquired by the store.

A teenage girl visits the table.
Asks him questions.

A woman approaches.
Stands at the table's edge.

She picks up a book.
Flips through most of it.

She listens to the conversation.
Between him and the girl.

The girl asks him about writing.
He gives her a writing answer.

She tells him she's quitting volleyball.
So she can write more.

He tells her to re-consider.
To keep playing.

They talk some more.
The girl moves on.

Satisfied with what she heard.
The woman asks him to sign the book.

She says thank you.
Disappears in the bookstore.

Other shoppers stop.
Visit him at the table.

A teenage son with his father.
A retired couple.

A mother with her children.
A young man.

His chair faces the check-out line.
He sees the listening woman.

She's waiting.
Standing in a long line.

The line winds several rows.
Extends into the store's center.

She's occupied.
Her head is down.

His book is in her hands.
She's reading his best.

She doesn't pick up her head.
Doesn't stop reading.

She follows the line.
Turning pages.

Her movements.
Meager.

Her mind.
Caught in a story.

She's a stranger.
Getting to know him.

She buys the book.
Nothing else.

Her unspoken review.
Incomplete.

She walks to the store's exit.
The book in a crisp bag.

An early fan of his.
She convinces him it's all real.

He's an author.

28

Carefree

He walks into a gas station.
The nicest one in town.

His hair is wet.
Dripping sweat.

His eyebrows are wet.
Catching sweat.

His eyeglasses are wet.
Sliding from sweat.

His face is wet.
Glistening sweat.

His lips are dry.
Asking for water.

His shirt is wet.
Covered with sweat.

His right arm is weak.
Overused.

His back muscles are straining.
Failing.

His side muscles are tangled.
Trying.

His shorts are wet.
Pressed with sweat.

His legs aren't responding.
Their rhythm is broken.

His socks are wet.
Lined with sweat.

His sneakers are wet.
Laced with sweat.

His feet are trailing.
Ignored.

He's done.
Hitting tennis balls for hours.

A cold drink awaits in the back.
A reward.

He adds ice to a cup.
A fountain drink.

He walks to the check-out.
Stands in line.

Someone stares at his hobbled arrival.
Wonders if he's injured.

A couple of kids stare at him.
His wet shirt.

Someone senses he's wet.
Stares at him to make sure.

He smiles at each of them.
Adjusts his hat.

His mind is firing.
Electric.

He raises the cup to his mouth.
Takes a sip of his drink.

His body tells him it's okay.
It's over.

You can be nothing.
Do nothing.

You can think of nothing.

29

Humility

He's talking about himself.
He has to.

He's being interviewed.
Being asked about his art.

They ask about his book.
Writing.

The stories.
What he learned.

His reasons.
Process.

Few ask about his book.
Talking about it is unusual.

He answers for the interviewer.
The interview.

Some other writers.
Readers.

Himself.
The lost record.

Every answer is deliberate.
Complete.

He senses the inevitable question.
A self-assessment of his art.

It's a rare public chance.
Improbable.

He recalls how he was.
When people asked him questions.

About abilities he might possess.
Qualities he might possess.

Whatever he was given.
Tried to use.

He deflected the questions.
Minimized himself.

His proper responses drew more comments.
Predictable praise.

He wasn't great, he thought.
Why talk about himself.

The interviewer delivers the chance.
Invites a real response.

"When you look at what you wrote, what do you
think?" the interviewer says.

Don't.
Don't boast.

It's not likable.
Not done.

Act.
Pretend to have no idea.

"One of my intentions was for the writing to be high quality," he says.
"I think each chapter reaches that level. As an objective writer, I do know what I wrote."

"Of course, it's for people to decide now."

30

Trust

He hears his teenage kid.
They walk downstairs.

They pass him in the living room.
Enter the kitchen.

They get what they need.
Start making a sandwich.

They announce they're leaving.
Will be back later.

It's almost sunset.
Dark soon.

He gets up.
Stands between rooms.

He asks where.
Who with.

They say a couple possibilities.
Some names.

He says it's a blessing to have friends.
Places to go.

They enter the dining room.
Sit to eat their sandwich.

He takes position in the kitchen.
Cleans up the counters.

They say they like the sauce.
Ask if he can get more.

He says sure.
He'll get it next time.

They offer another detail.
About the night.

They may meet up later.
With another group of friends.

He asks which group.
Where.

They say some names.
They don't know yet.

He says that's great.
They don't see that group much.

They say yeah.
Their group is hanging with other groups more.

He's stated facts before.
The few rules.

He's repeated them.
They know them.

He makes no statements.
Not tonight.

They finish eating.
Clear their place.

They wash their hands.
Collect a few items around the house.

They head to the front door.
Hold it open.

Bye, they yell.
Closing the door.

He hears them leave.
Rushes out of the kitchen.

He walks out the front door.
Stands on the top step.

He watches them look young.
It's a nice night, he says.

Be yourself.

31

Peace

He sits down to finish writing.
He has to.

A scene is nearly done.
He's moments away.

A distant vision he visited.
Now words.

The picture.
Clear.

The story.
Life.

The distractions.
Cut.

He won't be long.
It's a light session.

A few words are waiting.
Are they worthy.

He's swift.
Makes final decisions.

No letter is stray.
Each one belongs.

The scene is complete.
It needs him no more.

It is the best of him.
A written vision.

He rises.
A poet again.

He wants nothing.
Needs nothing.

For a day.
He's free.

His poem tells him so.

32

Immaterial

He walks into a department store.
A gift card is in his pocket.

The card's loaded with cash.
A generous gift.

He's determined to spend the card.
Inside the actual store.

There are thousands of goods.
Something for everyone.

He walks the entire store.
Every section.

What about this shirt.
He has shirts.

What about these pants.
He has pants.

What about these shoes.
He has shoes.

He sees someone picking a shirt.
The latest fashion.

What about this gadget.
He doesn't want a gadget.

What about this watch.
He doesn't want a watch.

What about this tool.
He doesn't want a tool.

He sees someone picking a gadget.
The latest technology.

What about this game.
He doesn't play games anymore.

What about this football.
He doesn't play football anymore.

What about this box of candy.
He doesn't eat candy anymore.

He sees someone picking a game.
The latest title.

Is there nothing he wants.
Why can't he want anything.

He passes people in the check-out line.
Wanting something.

He leaves the store.
The unused gift card in his pocket.

He passes people entering the store.
Wanting something.

There's nothing he wants in the store.
No store has what he wants.

What he wants isn't for sale.

33

Honor

He's moving around his house.
From room to room.

What should he write next.
He doesn't know.

After lunch.
Light swings of a tennis racket.

He's given an answer.
A moment.

He remembers all of it.
Exactly what happened.

It was long ago.
A different time.

He was younger.
The same.

It involved a girl he knew once.
A small cast.

He could write it.
As it was.

He could make it real.
A second time.

It would be natural.
Halting.

It would wow.
Hearts would quicken.

What happens to them.
People would ask.

It would work.
He's certain.

He's tempted.
Why not.

It's not crude.
Not vengeful.

He lounges on the living room couch.
Looks into the back yard.

He stays there.
Waiting to accept it.

It would defy his doctrine.
What he admired as a boy.

What he could write.
He won't write.

It would be careless now.
Reckless.

It could never be beauty.

34

Honesty

He opens the door to a restaurant.
His wife enters first.

He approaches the hostess.
A table for two please.

They follow to their table.
Pick their chairs.

They settle themselves.
Look around the place.

A server visits them.
They give their drink orders.

They examine the menu.
Discuss their options.

He says the salads look good.
The sides look interesting.

She says they should get an appetizer.
One to share.

The server returns.
They reply with their meal orders.

They wait.
Sitting across from each other.

He says he likes the music.
Likes the art.

She says she's happy about her order.
Looking forward to her fish.

He says their walk earlier was long.
Great for their appetites.

She says she likes her iced tea.
Asks if he wants to try some.

He prepares to break a rule.
To talk about what's serious.

Who is she today.
At the table.

He leans his head to one side.
Looks at her.

Can you tell me something, he says.
Is there anything that's bothering you.

Anything you want.
For yourself.

I don't know, she says.
Where would I begin.

There's so much going on.
Let's not right now.

It's fine, he says.
I want to hear it.

Why, she says.
You already know all of it.

I don't, he says.
How could I.

I want to know what you think about.

35

Potential

He wants to go somewhere.
Do something.

It's a place he believes exists.
He needs to find out.

He doesn't have to go.
No one is going with him.

He must complete the labyrinth first.
The mind game many never stop playing.

He begins by looking at pictures.
Turns to reading.

He turns to watching.
To listening.

He turns to history.
To the future.

He turns to athletes.
To entertainers.

He turns to professionals.
To specialists.

He turns to chatter.
To delusions.

He turns to spending.
To getting.

He turns to food.
To drink.

He turns to vice.
To weakness.

He turns to family.
To friends.

He passes all of them.
They can't take him there.

He finishes the labyrinth.
There's still time.

He reaches the place.
It's unadorned.

There's nothing to consume.
He's alone.

He can't go back.
Stay here, he thinks.

He wants to know who he is.
There's no other way.

He sits at a table.
Starts writing.

He will become what is possible.

36

Communication

He sees his wife after dinner.
She's in the living room.

Sitting on the couch.
Alone.

She's reading on her device.
Messaging family.

He cleans up his dinner plate.
The kitchen some.

He walks into their bedroom to change.
Get more comfortable clothes.

He sits down on their bed.
Recalls last night.

Their serious talk at a restaurant.
They said what they've been thinking.

They stated what they expect.
What they need.

What can change.
What would tighten their bond.

He hears noise from the living room.
Sounds from the big screen.

It's a channel she likes.
It's starting.

He used to watch it with her.
They'd talk.

He doesn't want to watch.
He wants to do something else.

He leaves their bedroom.
Heads to the kitchen.

He gets a drink.
Walks into the living room.

He sits on the couch.
Near her.

What are you doing, she says.
Are you going to watch.

I'm sitting here with you, he says.
Is that okay.

Of course, she says.
It's just been a while.

There's room for their dog.
They invite their dog up.

Their dog jumps on the couch.
Lies between them.

He pets their dog.
Reaches across their dog.

He takes her hand.
She lets him.

He lays their hands on their dog.
Still.

They sit together.
Say nothing.

For another show.
For another night.

They're a couple.

37

Hope

He could be down.
Defeated.

He could ask why.
Why now.

Anyone would be weak.
Less.

He's not.
He can't be.

He's going to write a play.
Produce a play.

He tells his wife.
His daughter.

He tells his older son.
His younger son.

The unwritten play is him.
His future.

Searching.
He'll find the play's meaning.

Alone.
He'll visit the play's characters.

Silent.
He'll tell the play's story.

Doubting.
He'll believe the play's ending.

There's a missing piece.
The performance.

He asks an actor for help.
She says yes.

To actors for the play.
A director.

To co-producing the play.
A theater.

He can see the actors acting.
The audience listening.

He can't plead for more.
For something else.

There's no time to be ungrateful.
He has a new dream.

He has a play to write.

38

Gratitude

He enters a fast-food restaurant.
His teenage son follows.

Their entrance is noticed.
Youthful.

He passes a high table with stools.
It's empty.

The spacious tabletop is fake wood.
Different from the rest.

He walks back.
Throws his jacket there to save it.

They weave the line to order lunch.
It's their turn.

"I'm sure you know what you want," he says.
"You order first. Don't get everything on the
menu."

His son scans the entire menu above.
Orders a list of familiar foods.

"Just order something good," his son says.
"You should get some fries."

He orders a drink.
An ice cream cone.

His son adds an ice cream cone.
Inspired by the idea.

"I have a table," he says.
"It's the best one."

They sit at the high table.
Across from each other.

A worker delivers a strawberry sundae they didn't order.
They've never seen such a sundae.

They both smile at the whipped cream.
Maybe they could eat it.

A different worker brings out their order.
A tray of food for his son.

His son starts to eat.
He starts to talk.

They talk about school.
Sports.

Friends.
Girls.

Plans.
Life.

They hear an older man talking near them.
Another man responds from across the restaurant.

The older men know each other from town.
Keep talking across the crowded restaurant.

"They're really going to have a whole conversation
like that," his son says.
"Yelling over everyone."

His son is smiling.
Amazed at their defiance.

"I love it," he says.
"They haven't seen each other in a while."

His son finishes his food.
Smiles about what's coming.

"I'm getting a refill," he says.
"Don't go anywhere."

He leaves the table.
Returns with a new drink.

He doesn't want their lunch to end.

39

Solitude

He's listening to classical music.
Modern composers.

He glances at a clock.
Notes the time.

He wants to understand himself.
His existence.

What matters.
What's beautiful.

He starts writing.
A few words appear.

He writes whatever's next.
Lines appear.

He follows the music.
A scene appears.

His rhythm slows.
His thinking slows.

It's gone.
He's unsure.

He looks out a window.
Watches a flag sail.

He could stop.
He wants to stop.

Stay.
There's more to uncover.

More to know.
More to understand.

He returns.
Composes more.

He sees it.
He hears it.

The scene is different.
Better than before.

He could continue.
Stay.

He looks at the clock.
His session is done.

He's in a chair at a game table.
He doesn't play the game.

A classical song is playing.
Evoking him.

He keeps seeing himself somewhere else.
Away from where he sits.

He's with other writers.
Debating.

He's with new writers.
Teaching.

He's with readers.
Listening.

He's a writer they know.
A writer who's smiling.

He's a writer who isn't alone.

40

Beauty

He parks his car on a street.
Checks his hair in the mirror.

He grabs his grocery bag in the back.
Studies a house from the sidewalk.

He follows the walkway in.
Avoids jagged bushes.

He stops to pull up his pants.
Tighten his belt.

He reaches for a stick of gum.
Puts it in his mouth.

He hears music in the house.
What are they listening to.

His grocery bag hits a statue.
The mythical creature is fine.

He walks up steps to the front door.
Halts for a holiday wreath.

He sees people moving in the house.
Who are they.

He pushes the doorbell.
Hears a pleasant chime.

He waits a while.
Switches the grocery bag to his other hand.

Should he ring the bell again.
Not yet.

The door opens.
He glimpses inside the house.

His new friend stands in the doorway.
One step higher.

They smile at him.
Declare his name.

All right, they say.
We were hoping you'd make it.

They move to the side.
Hold the door open for him.

Come in man.

Thank you to these special people for their support of me and this book: my wife, my kids, my parents, my siblings, and my extended family.

Without you, there are no stories.
With you, there is sub-life.

SUBPARTS OF A LIFE

CHRIS EHRLICH

Chris Ehrlich is an original (human) author, entrepreneur, husband, dad of 3 young adults, and tennis hacker. He holds a degree in English and political science from Denison University. He's lived in Michigan, Ohio, California, and Oregon. He writes in Tennessee.

www.ingramcontent.com/pod-product-compliance
Lightning Source LLC
Chambersburg PA
CBHW070326130626
46556CB00007B/2747